Learning & Caring About
OUR SELVES

By Gayle Bittinger

Illustrated by Kathy Kotomaimoce

Warren Publishing House, Inc.
Everett, Washington

Editorial Staff:
    Kathleen Cubley, Brenda Lalonde, Elizabeth McKinnon,
    Jean Warren, Erica West

Production Staff:
    Manager: Eileen Carbary; *Assistant:* Jo Anna Brock
    Book and Cover Design, Computer Graphics: Kathy Kotomaimoce
    Cover Computer Graphics: Eric Stovall

ISBN 0-911019-51-0

Library of Congress Catalog Card Number 91-67076
Printed in the United States of America
Published by: Warren Publishing House, Inc.
        P.O. Box 2250
        Everett, WA 98203

20 19 18 17 16 15 14 13 12 11 10 9 8 7 6 5 4 3

Introduction

Our Selves is filled with over 120 fun, easy and inexpensive art, language, game, movement, music and snack activities to help young children learn and care about themselves and others.

The book includes activities for developing your children's self-awareness, enhancing their self-esteem and encouraging them to identify and express their feelings. There are opportunities for your children to learn about their bodies and how to take care of them through activities about body parts, appropriate touching, good health habits, dental hygiene and nutrition. There are also activities for helping children learn about friends, families and strangers; plus activities to promote sharing and caring with others.

Each chapter is followed by reproducible parent flyers with activities for parents and children to do together. The reproducible patterns at the end of the book are provided for your convenience.

Helping young children learn to take care of themselves and to appreciate their special qualities is the first step in helping them learn to take care of and appreciate others.

Gayle Bittinger

Contents

Getting to Know

OURSELVES

All About Me Posters

Make a poster for each child and attach his or her photo to it. Let the children add their handprints to their posters in the colors of their choice. Display the posters on a wall in your room. Throughout the year add additional items about the children to their posters. Tie these items in with stories, units or special occasions that occur throughout the year. (Also be sure to include the children's birthdays, families, favorite colors, favorite foods, heights and weights, favorite things to do, special skills, etc.). These posters are very popular in the room and are well-received by parents at the end of the year. But most of all, they make the children feel special!

All About Me Books

Help the children make books about themselves over a period of time. Each day give them each a piece of paper with a different title on it, such as "My Favorite Foods," "My Favorite Color," "My Family," "My Favorite Toys." Have the children decorate their pages with crayon drawings or glued-on magazine pictures. Put each child's book pages together. Add a construction paper cover with the title "All About Me" and a photo of the child on the front of it.

Who Am I?

Give each child crayons and a doll shape cut out of posterboard. Set out several mirrors around the room. Let the children look in the mirrors to discover their hair and eye colors and other special features. Then have them color their posterboard dolls to look just like themselves. Tell them to make their dolls as special as they are. Hang the dolls in a row around the room with hands touching. This activity provides an excellent opportunity for discussing similarities and differences while pointing out how each child is unique and special. Try doing this at the beginning of the year and at the end to show the children and their parents how much the children's self-concepts changed over the year.

Picture Me

You will need a snapshot of each child. (Make photocopies of the snapshots so you can do this activity again and again.) Have the children draw pictures of things that interest them (a bus, a person on a horse, a flower, a swimming pool, etc.). When the children are finished, cut a hole in an appropriate part of each child's picture and tape in its place a photocopy of the child's snapshot. This makes for fun, and occasionally humorous, pictures. Children love to see these pictures of themselves!

"Getting to Know Me" Box

Cover a small shoebox with wrapping paper and call it the "Getting to Know Me" box. Each day send the box home with a different child. Have the child bring back the box the next day filled with some of his or her special things, such as a favorite toy, snapshots of family members or pets, or anything else that is important to the child. At group time let the child share the items in the box to explain who he or she is and what makes him or her special.

My Own Snack

Cut fruits and vegetables into bite-sized pieces. Put each kind of fruit or vegetable in a separate serving bowl with a serving spoon. Give each child a small empty bowl. Let the children choose which fruits and vegetables they want to eat and spoon a little of each one into their bowls.

Thumbs Up, Thumbs Down

This activity fosters awareness of self and others and explores some of the ways in which we are the same and different. Have the children sit in a circle and practice the thumbs-up response (Yes, hurray!) and the thumbs-down response (No, yuk!). Then have the children respond accordingly when you ask such yes or no questions as these: "Did you play with blocks today? Are you wearing blue? Do you like hamburgers? Do you have a sister?"

Favorite Things

Sung to: "Skip to My Lou"

I like kittens, what about you?
I like kittens, what about you?
I like kittens, what about you?
What about you, my darling?

Let the children suggest the names of other favorite things to substitute for the word *kittens*.

Mildred Hoffman

Journals

Staple several sheets of construction paper together to make a journal for each child. Set aside a special time each day for the children to draw or write in their journals or to dictate stories for you to write in them. If desired, offer a topic each day for the children to consider, such as: "What did you do last night? What makes you happy? What is your favorite game?"

People Center

Arrange a small area in the room to put materials that can be used for enhancing self-concept. Suggested materials include mirrors, paper and crayons for drawing self-portraits; snapshots of the children and their families; snapshots of the children when they were younger; scales for the children to weigh themselves on; and a growth chart on a wall to use for measuring heights.

I Am Special
Sung to: "Twinkle, Twinkle, Little Star"

I am special, yes I am,
In my way, I am a star.
I have my own special smile,
And my own special style.
I am special, yes I am,
In my way, I am a star.

Barbara B. Fleisher

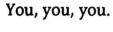

You, You, You,
Sung to: "Three Blind Mice"

You, you, you; you, you, you.
We like you, we like you.
There's no one else in the world just like you.
You're special, you know, and we care about you.
Just look at all the great things you can do.
You, you, you.

Diane Thom

Special Person of the Week

At the beginning of each week, select a child to be the Special Person of the Week. Take an instant photo of the child and interview him or her at circle time. Put all the information on a piece of posterboard along with the photo. Use a combination of words and symbols to tell about the special person. Write the person's name and age in large letters and numbers. Then draw stick figures to show the number of people and pets in his or her family. Add a paper circle of the person's favorite color and a magazine or catalog picture of his or her favorite activity or toy. The special person can have special privileges for the week, such as being first in line or feeding the fish. At the end of the week, give the child the poster to take home.

My Favorite Book

Assign each child a different day to bring in a favorite book to share. Post the dates on a calendar and send a reminder note home with the child the night before it is his or her turn. The book the child brings should take ten minutes or less to read. Let the child who brought the book sit next to you while you read it to the group at storytime.

Variation: Let the children choose favorite books from those you have in your reading corner.

"You Are Special" Awards

Make photocopies of the "You Are Special" Award Certificate on page 74. Give out "You Are Special" awards to several children each day. Explain why you are giving out the awards. For example: "Alyssa learned how to pump her legs on the swing; Andrew helped clean-up today; Katie built a house with the blocks today."

Group Album

Collect a photo of each child and each adult helper. Glue each photo on a separate piece of paper. Put the pages together with two extra pages at the beginning and some extra pages at the end. On the first page write "(Name of group)'s Album." Reserve the second page for the "authors" of the album to write their names. Have each person find his or her picture in the album and draw or write something about him or herself. Use the extra pages at the end for volunteers and new children coming into your group. Keep the album out so that it can be looked at during appropriate times.

Most Important Person in the World

Collect a small box with an attached lid, such as a school supplies box or a cigar box, and a mirror that fits inside the box. Glue the mirror in the bottom of the box. Show the box to a child and ask him or her a question such as: "Who is the most important person in the world? Who draws the best pictures in the world? Who is a very special child?" Then have the child open the box and look in the mirror to discover the answer to the question.

Mirror, Mirror

While you read the following poem out loud, have each child look into a mirror and act out the motions described.

I look in the mirror and who do I see?
A very wonderful, special me!
    (Point to self.)
With pretty eyes all shiny and bright,
    (Point to eyes.)
My smile shows my teeth, all pearly white.
    (Smile and point to teeth.)
It certainly is great to be
This very wonderful, special ME!
    (Hug self.)

Ann M. O'Connell

Birth Certificates

Make a photocopy of the Birth Certificate on page 75 for each child. Fill in the child's full name and date of birth. Have each child bring in a small baby picture to attach to his or her certificate, if desired. Talk with the children about what it was like when they were babies. If possible, have a baby brought in to visit your group. Then give each child his or her birth certificate.

Measuring Up

Measure the heights of the children at the beginning of the year. At the end of the year, measure them again. Make an award "medal" out of construction paper for each child.

Write in the child's name and how much he or she has grown over the year. Then attach a length of ribbon that measures the same number of inches he or she has grown.

Feelings Lotto

Make several sets of Feelings Lotto games. To make each set, divide two large index cards into six sections each. Draw six different feeling faces, such as happy, sad, surprised, mad, scared and tired, in the sections on one card for a gameboard. Draw six matching feelings faces in the sections on the second card. Then cut out the sections to make game cards. Store each game in a separate envelope. To play, have the children take turns placing the game cards on top of the matching sections on the gameboards.

Happy Eggs, Sad Eggs

For each child cut two large egg shapes out of construction paper. Draw a happy face on one shape and a sad face on the other. Pass out the egg shapes. Then make up statements that children would think of as happy or sad, such as, "I met a friendly egg today," or "I fell and hurt my shell." As you make each statement, have the children hold up either their happy egg faces or their sad ones.

Variation: Instead of egg shapes, use pumpkin shapes, turkey shapes, heart shapes, etc.

Happy Book

Have the children draw pictures of themselves doing what makes them feel the happiest. Have each child dictate a short description for you to write at the top or bottom of his or her drawing. Laminate each drawing (or cover it with clear self-stick paper). Punch holes in the left-hand sides of the drawings and fasten them together with metal rings. Add a cover titled "Happy Book," if desired. Read your Happy Book at circle time and display it on a shelf in your library corner.

Feelings Puppets

Make a simple puppet for each of several emotions. Also cut out magazine pictures of people expressing those emotions. Have the children sit in a circle with the magazine pictures in the center. Hold up one of the puppets. Ask the children to tell you how that puppet is feeling. Then ask them to find the pictures of people they think are feeling the same way. Discuss why people might feel that way. Repeat with the remaining puppets.

Simon Says "Feelings"

Play Simon Says with the children, substituting feeling phrases for the usual directions. For example, say: "Simon says, `Look happy,'" or "Simon says, `Look angry,'" or "Simon says, `Look brave.'" In between commands ask the children questions about those feelings, such as: "What makes you feel happy? What makes you feel angry? When do you feel brave?"

Feelings Masks

Set out materials for making masks, such as paper plates, paper bags, construction paper scraps, yarn, glue, crayons and felt-tip markers. Have the children use the materials to make Feeling Masks. Let each child make as many masks as he or she wishes. Have the children wear their masks when you talk about feelings.

Feelings

Sung to: "Twinkle, Twinkle, Little Star"

Sometimes on my face you'll see,
How I feel inside of me.
A smile means happy, a frown means sad,
And when I grit my teeth I'm mad.
When I'm proud I beam and glow,
But when I'm shy my head hangs low.

Have the children act out the feelings as they
are described in the song.

Karen Folk

I'll Hug You

Sung to: "The Farmer in the Dell"

I'll hug you when you're sad,
I'll hug you when you're glad,
I'll hug you when you're feeling scared,
I'll hug you when you're mad.

Betty Silkunas

Exploring Moods

Have the children dance, move, paint or color to music of different moods. Talk about the moods that the music suggests. Extend the activity by asking the children to make up happy, sad or angry songs.

Feelings Pockets

Fold the bottom of a piece of construction paper halfway up to make a pocket. Fasten the sides together. Draw a simple face showing a feeling on the front of the pocket. Make as many pockets as desired, depending on the age and skill of your children. Cut out magazine pictures that show people in a variety of situations. Mount the pictures on lightweight cardboard or construction paper and cover them with clear self-stick paper for durability. Hang the Feelings Pockets on a wall.

Place the magazine pictures facing down in front of the pockets. Let one child at a time pick up a picture, tell what is happening in it and describe how the person in the picture is feeling. Then have the child put the picture into the corresponding feeling pocket. Make sure the children understand that there are no right or wrong responses. This activity provides a wonderful opportunity to discuss and show acceptance of differences in people's feelings.

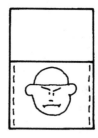

Paper Tear

Unfold sheets of newspaper and put them in a pile in the middle of the floor. Have each child take a sheet of the newspaper. Then say, "Show me how you would tear your newspaper if you were feeling happy." The children then tear their newspapers "happily," taking new sheets of paper as they like. After a while, change the mood to mad, sad, frustrated or any other feeling you have been talking about. Be sure to include a final,

"Show me how you would put the newspaper into the garbage can if you were feeling _____."

Feelings Cube

Select a cube of wood, a plastic photo cube or a small square cardboard box. Attach a picture of a feelings face to each side of the cube. (Repeat faces, if necessary, for younger children.) Have the children sit in a circle. Choose one child to start. Let that child roll the cube like a die. When the cube stops, have the child name the feeling on the face that comes up and make a face showing that feeling. Then have all the children show that same feeling. Finally, let the child who rolled the cube tell about a time when he or she felt that way. Continue playing the game until everyone has had a turn.

Feelings Board

Draw simple feelings faces down the left-hand side of a piece of wood and insert nails or hooks in a row beside each face. Write each child's name on an index card and punch a hole in the top of it. As the children arrive, or during circle time, have each child hang his or her name on a nail or hook beside the face that best describes how he or she is feeling. Let the children move their names during the day as their feelings change. At circle time, you and the children can count the number of children feeling happy, sad, mad, etc. Talk about how feelings change and why someone might feel happy or mad.

Variation: Adapt this activity for use on a flannelboard.

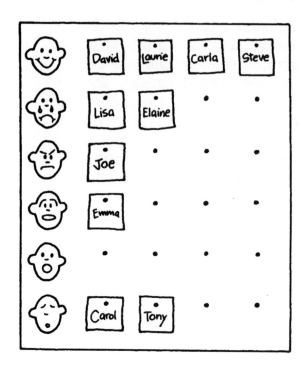

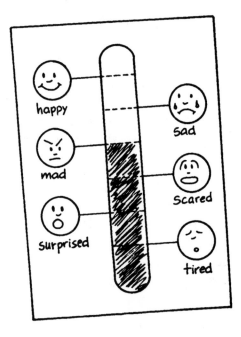

Feelings Thermometers

Make photocopies of the Feelings Thermometer on page 76. Every day, give each child a thermometer. Have the children color in the "mercury" on their thermometers until it stops by the picture that represents how they feel. Let them fill in new thermometers as their feelings change.

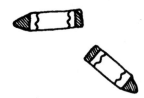

Feelings Books

Help the children make Feelings Books. Give each child four sheets of paper, each one labeled with a different feeling, such as "Happy," "Sad," "Angry" or "Mad." Let the children look through magazines for pictures of people with different expressions. Have them cut or tear out the pictures and paste them on the appropriate papers. Tie or staple each child's papers together to make a book.

Feelings Game

Prepare a list of situations such as the ones found below. Read each situation out loud and have the children show with their faces how they would feel. In some cases you may get the same reaction from all the children, while in others you might get a variety of responses.

How would you feel if

- your brother pushed you?
- your cousin was coming over to play?
- it was your birthday today?
- your balloon popped?
- it rained during your picnic?
- you got to help make cookies?
- your TV broke?
- you found a quarter?

I am happy when....

Feelings Phrase

On an extra-large piece of paper write a feeling phrase such as: "When I am angry, I...; I am scared when...; I am happy when...." Encourage the children to complete the phrase by drawing pictures on the paper or by dictating words for you to write down. Later, arrange a time to discuss all the responses.

Feelings Tape

Write out a feelings question like one of those that follow and place it near a tape recorder. One at a time, have the children record their answers to the question on tape. Play back the responses when all the children can listen to them.

How do you feel when

- someone pushes you down?
- you see someone crying?
- you get to stay up late?
- your best friend comes to play?

Dear Parents,

We are learning about ourselves and how special and unique each one of us is. Try the following activities with your child to discover something special about your child and yourself.

Special Box

Help your child find a small box, such as a shoebox, to make into his or her special box. Let your child decorate his or her box with wrapping paper, felt-tip markers, stickers, glitter, crayons, etc. Let your child use his or her box for keeping private, special things.

Handprints

Use a brush to put a light coating of paint on the palm of one of your child's hands. Have your child press his or her hand on a piece of paper. Then let your child use the brush to put paint on one of your hands. Make a handprint next to your child's. Compare your handprints. Talk about the things you liked to do when your hands were the size of your child's. Talk about the things your child would like to do when his or her hands are as big as yours.

Someone Special

Have your child look in a mirror while you read this poem to him or her.

I look in the mirror and who do I see?
A very wonderful, special me!
    (Point to self.)
With pretty eyes all shiny and bright,
    (Point to eyes.)
My smile shows my teeth, all pearly white.
    (Smile and point to teeth.)
It certainly is great to be
This very wonderful, special ME!
    (Hug self.)

Ann M. O'Connell

Dear Parents,

We are learning about how everyone starts out as a baby and becomes bigger and stronger and able to do more and more things. Do the following activities with your child to show how much growing he or she has done in just a few short years.

Time Line

On a long piece of paper draw a long line. At the beginning of the line put the date of your child's birth. Then as you talk with your child about important events in his or her life, mark them at the appropriate places on the time line. Let your child illustrate the events as desired.

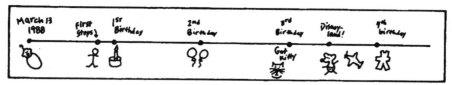

Growth Chart

Keep a growth chart for your child. On the first day of each month, weigh and measure your child and record his or her weight and height on your chart. Talk about how much your child has grown in one month, three months, one year.

Ashley's Growth Chart		
	WEIGHT	HEIGHT
January	35	42"
February	37	42½"

Growing Every Day

Sung to: "Twinkle, Twinkle, Little Star"

When I was a baby small,
I could only crawl, crawl, crawl.
Now I'm growing up so big,
I can run and dance a jig.
I am growing every day,
Growing up in every way.

Gayle Bittinger

Growing Tree

On a large piece of construction paper draw a simple tree shape that has one branch for every year old your child is plus one branch for the day he or she was born. (If your child is four, the tree should have five branches.) Cut out the tree shape and display it on a wall. On the lowest branch attach a picture of your child at birth. On the next lowest branch attach a picture of your child at one year. On the third lowest branch attach a picture of your child at two years, and so on. Talk to your child about how much he or she has grown.

Dear Parents,

We are learning about feelings. We are learning that everyone feels happy, sad, excited, lonely, angry or frustrated at one time or another. Do the following activities with your child to learn about and share feelings.

Puppet Talk

Make a hand puppet out of a paper bag or an old sock. Give the puppet to your child. Ask your child questions about feelings for the puppet to "answer." You could ask such questions as these: "How do you feel when it's time to go to bed? How do you feel when you play at Emily's house? What makes you feel the happiest?" (Children often express themselves more freely when talking through a puppet.) Then put the puppet on your hand and have your child asks you questions.

Feelings Face Toast

Make peanut butter toast with your child. Give your child raisins to put on the toast to make a feelings face (happy, sad, mad, etc.).

Today's Feelings

Draw simple faces with different feelings on them (or cut out magazine pictures of people showing different feelings). Each day have your child hang up on the refrigerator the face that best describes how he or she is feeling. If your child's feelings change during the day, have him or her change the face on the refrigerator. If desired, make a set of feeling faces for yourself, too.

I'll Hug You

Ask your child what it feels like to be sad, glad, scared or mad. Make sad, glad, scared and mad faces together. Then sing the following song together to remind each other that no matter what you're feeling, there is always someone around who loves you.

Sung to: "The Farmer in the Dell"

I'll hug you when you're sad,
I'll hug you when you're glad,
I'll hug you when you're feeling scared,
I'll hug you when you're mad.

Betty Silkunas

Getting to Know Ourselves Contributors

Ideas in this chapter were contributed by:

Janice Bodenstedt, Jackson, MI
Cindy Dingwall, Palatine, IL
Barbara B. Fleisher, Glen Oaks, NY
Karen Folk, Franklin, MA
Mildred Hoffman, Tacoma, WA
Joan Hunter, Elbridge, NY
Josephine Illick, Kempton, PA
Barbara H. Jackson, Denton, TX
Ann M. O'Connell, Coaldale, PA
Beverly Qualheim, Marquette, MI
Susan M. Paprocki, Northbrook, IL
Betty Silkunas, Lansdale, PA
Connie Jo Smith, Bowling Green, KY
Jane M. Spannbauer, So. St. Paul, MN
Diane Thom, Maple Valley, WA
Kathleen Tobey, Griffith, IN
Kristine Wagoner, Puyallup, WA

OUR BODIES

Body Picture

Give the children photocopies of the Body Outline pattern on page 77. Have each child complete a picture to look like him or herself by adding the right hair color, hair length, eye color, clothes, etc. Then name different body parts and have the children point to them on their pictures.

Perfume Fun

Set out two bottles of perfume or cologne. Have the children come up to you, one at a time. Let them select which perfume or cologne they want you to put on them. Then have them name and point to the body part where they want the perfume or cologne.

Flannelboard Fun

Cut a child's body shape out of felt. Cut the body shape into head, chest, arms, legs, feet and hands sections. Put the sections together on a flannelboard. Let the children take the body sections apart and put them together again while naming them.

Touch Your Nose

Sung to: "Row, Row, Row Your Boat"

Touch, touch, touch your nose,
And then touch your toes.
Clap your hands and stomp your feet,
And touch your nose again.

Touch, touch, touch your wrist,
And then make a fist.
Clap your hands and stomp your feet,
And touch your wrist again.

Touch, touch, touch your lips,
And then touch your hips.
Clap your hands and stomp your feet,
And touch your lips again.

Touch, touch, touch your eyes,
And then touch your thighs.
Clap your hands and stomp your feet,
And touch your eyes again.

Dawn Thimm

Body Parts

Have the children divide into pairs. Ask one child in each pair to lie on the floor. Then have the partner gently follow directions such as these: "Move your friend's arm; Bend your friend's leg; Touch your friend's ear; Shake your friend's hand; Tickle your friend's fingers; Touch your friend's knee." Then have the children switch places and repeat the activity.

Variation: Have the children follow directions like these: "Touch your hand to your friend's foot; Touch your wrist to your friend's knee; Touch your nose to your friend's tummy; Touch your ear to your friend's arm; Touch your fingers to your friend's head; Touch your elbow to your friend's shoulder."

Tap Your Head

Have the children act out the motions as you read the poem below.

Tap your head,
Tap your toe,
Turn in a circle,
Bend down low.
Tap your nose,
Tap your knees,
Hands on your shoulders,
Sit down, please.

Margery Kranyik

Finger Play

Gently tape together all of the fingers on one of each child's hands. Encourage the children to play for a while. Then have the children talk about how it feels to have their fingers taped together. Ask them to tell you what things are hard for them to do and what things they can't do at all. Then take the tape off their fingers and have them tell you all the things fingers can do.

Elbows and Knees

Explain to the children that every body part has a special function, even something like an elbow or a knee that seems insignificant. Then have the children move their elbows. Ask: "What would we do if we had no elbows and could not bend our arms?" Have the children try showing how they would eat, how they would button their shirts or how they would brush their hair. (They would not be able to do these tasks.) Then have the children move their knees. Ask them what they would do if they had no knees and could not bend their legs. Have them try jumping without bending their knees. Let them try sitting down on the floor without bending their knees.

Loving Touches

Explain to the children that loving touches are hugs, pats on the back and other touches that are positive and healthy. Everyone needs loving touches, but we all have the right to say if we want to be touched or not. Ask the children if they can think of some loving touches. Then sing the following song.

Sung to: "Skip to My Lou"

I'll give you some loving touches,
I'll give you some loving touches,
I'll give you some loving touches
That we can both enjoy.

I'll stop if you do not like them,
I'll stop if you do not like them,
I'll stop if you do not like them
'Cause you are not a toy.

Ellen Hokanson

What If?

Have the children sit in a circle. Tell them that you are going to play a game that will help them know what to do if a person or a pet touches them in a way that hurts or is uncomfortable. Then ask the children the following questions after explaining that the answers are "No, don't touch me," "No, I don't like it," or "No, I won't touch you."

What would you do if

*   your aunt ruffled your hair too hard?
*   your dog jumped on you and knocked you down?
*   your friend tickled you so long that you cried?
*   someone you didn't know wanted you to give him or her a kiss?
*   your sister pulled your hair really hard?
*   your babysitter picked you up and hugged you when you wanted to play?
*   your kitty scratched you?
*   your little brother kicked you?
*   your dad teased you by rubbing his whiskery chin on your arm and you didn't like it?
*   your mom's friend wanted to give you a goodbye kiss and you didn't want one?

Afterward, let the children practice the answers together. Encourage the children to use loud voices and to say the answers like they mean them.

Run, Run, Run in Place

Sung to: "Row, Row, Row Your Boat"

Run, run, run in place
While you sing this song.
That's the way to help your heart
Stay healthy and grow strong.

Additional Verses: Jump, jump, up and down; Swing, swing, swing your arms; Walk, walk, walk around; etc.

Marian Berry

Listen to the Heartbeats

Bring in a stethoscope and let the children use it to listen to one another's hearts. Ask them to try describing the sound that the heart makes as it beats ("lub-dub, lub-dub"). Let them listen to one another's hearts while sitting quietly, then after doing jumping jacks. What differences can they hear in the heartbeats? Talk about how our hearts need both rest and exercise in order to stay healthy and strong.

Your Healthy Body

Sung to: "The Farmer in the Dell"

Your body has many parts,
Your body has many parts.
The parts work together
To make a healthy you.

Your heart pumps the blood,
Your heart pumps the blood.
The parts work together
To make a healthy you.

Additional Verses: Your lungs breathe in air;
Your teeth chew the food; Your stomach
digests the food; etc.

Janice Bodenstedt

Health Care Learning Center

Set up a Health Care Learning
Center in your room. Supply it with
a variety of items that have to do
with health care, such as a stethoscope, an eye chart, a scale, pictures
of doctors' and dentists' offices, etc.
Let the children explore and play
with the items.

Good Health Game

Place a variety of good health items on a tray, such as a comb, a brush, a washcloth, a bar of soap, a facial tissue, a jump rope and an apple. Have the children sit in a circle. Ask them how they feel when they are healthy and how they feel when they are not. Then let each child in turn select an item from the tray, tell how it helps him or her stay healthy and place the item in the middle of the circle.

Healthy Charades

Have the children sit in a circle. Ask one child to stand up. In the child's ear, whisper the name of an activity that promotes good health, such as washing hands, brushing teeth, using facial tissue, eating nutritious foods, resting properly or getting exercise. Then have the child act out the healthy activity and let the other children try guessing what it is. Continue until each child has had a chance to act out a healthy activity.

Sharing Boxes

Show the children a ball and a toothbrush. Ask them to tell which one would not be healthy to share and to explain why. (The toothbrush would not be healthy to share because it is something people put in their mouths.) Then set out two boxes, one marked with a happy face and the words "Healthy to Share" and the other marked with a sad face and the words "Not Healthy to Share." Place some familiar objects next to the boxes, such as a crayon, a comb, a cup, a toy, a piece of paper, a block, a fork and a drinking straw. Let each child select an item and place it in the appropriate box.

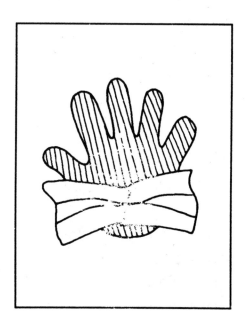

Tissue Power

Help each child trace around his or her hand on a piece of construction paper. Let the children cut out their hand shapes (or cut out the shapes yourself). Give each child another piece of construction paper and a facial tissue. Have the children glue their hand shapes to their papers and glue the tissues on top of their hand shapes. Display the completed papers around the room or near the facial tissue boxes to remind the children to use tissue when they need to wipe their noses.

Keep the Germs Away

Sung to: "The Mulberry Bush"

This is the way we cover our sneezes,
Cover our sneezes, cover our sneezes,
This is the way we cover our sneezes
To keep the germs away.

This is the way we wash our hands,
Wash our hands, wash our hands,
This is the way we wash our hands
To keep the germs away.

Susan M. Paprocki

Healthy Habits

Sung to: "Row, Row, Row Your Boat"

Eat, eat, from four food groups
To keep your body strong.
Too much candy, junk and pop
Does your body wrong.

Rest, rest, get good rest
Each and every night.
Feel perky in the morning
When your nighttime's right.

Wash, wash, both your hands
Use a lot of soap.
Don't give cold and flu germs
Any kind of hope.

Susan M. Paprocki

Achoo!

Sung to: "The Farmer in the Dell"

Achoo! Achoo! Achoo!
Achoo! Achoo! Achoo!
When you sneeze use tissue, please.
Achoo! Achoo! Achoo!

Becky Valenick

Cough or Sneeze

Sung to: "Mary Had a Little Lamb"

When you have to cough or sneeze,
Cough or sneeze, cough or sneeze,
When you have to cough or sneeze,
Cover your mouth, please.

We don't want to spread our germs,
Spread our germs, spread our germs,
We don't want to spread our germs,
Ah—ah—chooo!

Give each child a tissue to practice with as you sing the song.

Janice Bodenstedt

Tooth Puppets

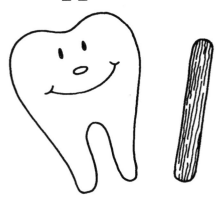
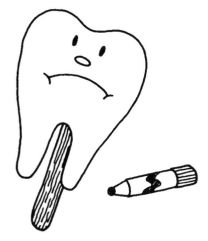

Use the Tooth pattern on page 78 as a guide for cutting tooth shapes out of white construction paper. Glue craft stick handles to the tooth shapes. Give each child a tooth puppet. Let the children draw happy faces on the fronts of their puppets and sad faces on the backs. Have the children hold their puppets. Make statements about dental care, such as: "Visit your dentist regularly; Eat lots of sweets; Brush your teeth only once a week; Floss your teeth every day." If the statement is something that would make their teeth "happy," have the children show you the happy faces on their tooth puppets. If the statement is something that would make their teeth "sad," have them show you the sad faces on their puppets.

Get My Toothpaste, Get My Brush

Sung to: "Twinkle, Twinkle, Little Star"

Get my toothpaste, get my brush,
I won't hurry, I won't rush.
Making sure my teeth are clean,
Front and back and in between.
When I brush for quite a while,
I will have a happy smile.

Frank Dally

Toothbrush Painting

Use the Tooth pattern on page 78 as a guide for cutting a large tooth shape out of white construction paper for each child. Have the children dip old toothbrushes into tempera paint "toothpaste" and then use them to "brush" their paper teeth. Show the children how to brush up and down, back and forth and in a circular motion. This is excellent practice for the real thing, but be sure to stress that the brushes and the pretend toothpaste should not be put into real mouths.

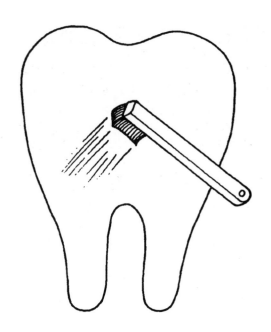

Tile Teeth

Fill several small containers with foods that will stain or stick to teeth, such as ketchup, grape juice and syrup. Place the containers on a table along with cotton swabs, small white ceramic tiles, old toothbrushes, toothpaste and two or three glasses of water. Let the children use the cotton swabs to spread small amounts of the foods on the ceramic tile "teeth." After the foods have dried, let the children remove them from their tiles by using the toothbrushes and toothpaste. Encourage the children to brush with up and down strokes and in circles. Have them dip their brushes in water as necessary. Explain that just as brushing the tiles gets the food off them, brushing their teeth after every meal cleans the food off and keeps their teeth healthy.

Platters of Health

Explain to the children that there are four food groups (milk and dairy products, fruits and vegetables, breads and grains, and meats and other proteins). Point out that our bodies need foods from each of these groups every day. Set out magazine pictures of nutritious foods from each of the groups. Give each child a paper plate to use for making a "Platter of Health." Have the children select pictures from each of the four food groups and glue them to their plates.

Shopping for Health

Collect a variety of empty cans and containers of nutritious foods (at least two for each child) and a few junk food cartons. Display the "foods" on a table or some shelves. Give the children shopping bags and let them each go shopping for one or two nutritious foods. Have the children sit in a circle after they have finished. One at a time, let them show the foods they bought and talk about the choices they made. If their choices include junk foods, discuss what junk food is and why they should not eat it all the time.

Four Food Groups
Sung to: "Frere Jacques"

Meats and proteins,
Breads and cereals,
Dairy too, dairy too.
Vegetables and fruits,
Vegetables and fruits.
Four food groups, four food groups.

Priscilla Starrett

Pick a Food
Sung to: "The Battle Hymn of the Republic"

Pick a food from each food group at every meal you eat,
Pick a food from each food group at every meal you eat,
Pick a food from each food group at every meal you eat,
And you'll grow up big and strong.

Refrain:

Meats and proteins are the first group,
Breads and cereals are the next group,
Dairy products are the third group,
And don't forget the vegetables and fruits!

Priscilla Starrett

Likes and Dislikes

Talk with the children about the foods they like and dislike. Talk about what they would do if they were served a food they didn't like. Then let them share their tastes in food by playing this game. On one side of your room hang up a picture you have drawn of "Love 'Em Lucy." On the other side of your room hang up another picture you have drawn of "Hate 'Em Harry."

Cut out magazine pictures of foods. Hold up a food picture. Have the children who really love that food stand close to Love 'Em Lucy, the children who really hate the food stand close to Hate 'Em Harry and the children who neither love the food nor hate it stand somewhere in between. Repeat with the remaining food pictures.

Nutritious Snacks

Set out foods from the four food groups, such as cheese cubes or cottage cheese, apple slices or carrot sticks, bread triangles or crackers and deviled ham or tuna salad. Then give each child a plate and let him or her choose one food from each of the four groups to eat for a snack.

Dear Parents,

We are learning about our bodies and how they move and work. Try doing the activities below with your child to explore more about your bodies together.

Mirroring

Sit or kneel in front of your child. Ask your child to slowly move his or her arms while you try to imitate the movement with your arms, without touching your child. Then reverse roles.

So Many Parts of Me
Sung to: "Twinkle, Twinkle, Little Star"

On my face I have a nose,
On my feet I have ten toes.
I've five fingers on each hand,
I am tall when I stand.
I have two eyes so I can see,
There are so many parts of me.

Diane Thom

Animal Moves

Share some physical activity with your child by doing the following animal moves.

Bear Walk — Place your hands on the floor in front of you and take giant bear steps with your hands and feet. Remember to growl like a bear. Keep a nose out for juicy berries.

Bunny Hop — While standing, bend your arms and let your wrists flop in front of your chest. Hop, hop, hop to the carrot patch.

Horse Kick — Squat down and place your hands on the floor in front of you. Kick your legs behind you. Try one leg at a time and then both at once. Be sure to support your weight on your arms and don't kick too high, you might fall. Whinny like a horse and watch out for breakable objects or furniture.

Dear Parents,

We are learning about how to take good care of our bodies. The following activities suggest a few of the many ways you and your child can treat your bodies well.

Choosing Snacks

Talk about choosing nutritious snacks over snacks that contain a lot of added sugar. Look through magazines together and tear or cut out pictures of healthy snacks and sugary snacks. Label one shoebox with a happy face and another with a sad face. Let your child sort the pictures into the appropriate boxes.

Incentive Chart

Pick a healthy habit that you and your child would like to practice every day, such as brushing teeth after each meal, exercising, or going to bed at a designated time. Make a chart with seven columns. Write a day of the week in each column. Divide the chart into two rows, one for your child and one for you. Every day that you or your child practice the healthy habit, put a sticker in the appropriate place. Plan a special reward for the end of the week if the chart is all filled up.

Healthy Habits

Sung to: "Row, Row, Row Your Boat"

Eat, eat, from four food groups
To keep your body strong.
Too much candy, junk and pop
Does your body wrong.

Rest, rest, get good rest
Each and every night.
Feel perky in the morning
When your nighttime's right.

Wash, wash, both your hands
Use a lot of soap.
Don't give cold and flu germs
Any kind of hope.

Susan M. Paprocki

Getting to Know Our Bodies Contributors

Ideas in this chapter were contributed by:

Marian Berry, Tacoma, WA
Janice Bodenstedt, Jackson, MI
Frank Dally, Ankeny, IA
Wes Epperson, Placerville, CA
Ann Herold-Short, Shelbyville, IN
Ellen Hokanson, Seattle, WA
Joan Hunter, Elbridge, NY
Debbie Jones, Richland, WA
Margery Kranyik, Hyde Park, MA
Joleen Meier, Marietta, GA
Susan M. Paprocki, Northbrook, IL
Connie Jo Smith, Bowling Green, KY
Priscilla Starrett, Warren, PA
Shari Steelsmith, Bothell, WA
Dawn Thimm, Balsam Lake, WI
Diane Thom, Maple Valley, WA
Kathleen Tobey, Griffith, IN
Becky Valenick, Rockford, IL
Anne Zipf, Metuchen, NJ

Getting to Know

OTHERS

Invite Table

A fun way to encourage children to mingle and to make new friends at the beginning of a school year is to have an Invite Table. Each day, tape a different child's name to the Invite Table. For that day, the child may invite any one child at a time to share the table's activities with him or her. At the beginning of the school year, you select the table's activities, such as blocks or play-dough. As the year progresses, the child in charge of the Invite Table may choose the activities to share.

Getting Acquainted Box

On index cards write such questions as these: "What do you like to do outside? What is your favorite color? What is your favorite thing to eat?" Put the cards in a box. Let the children take turns choosing a card from the box and giving it to you to read out loud. Have all of the children answer the question. This helps the children build relationships with one another by discovering similar likes and interests.

Wave Hello

Have the children sit in a circle. Sing the following song, substituting the name of one of your children for the name *Annie.* Have that child move to the center of the circle while you wave at him or her. Then have the child return to his or her place. Repeat for each child.

Sung to: "Frere Jacques"

Where is Annie, where is Annie?

Here she is, here she is.

Wave hello to Annie,

Wave hello to Annie.

There she goes, there she goes.

Betty Silkunas

Boys and Girls

Sung to: "Pop! Goes the Weasel"

All around Andrew,

The children circle slowly.

Andrew is clapping.

Clap, boys and girls!

Substitute the name of one of your children for the name *Andrew* and the name of the action your child is doing for the words *clapping* and *clap.*

Lois Putnam

Photo Memory Game

Take two pictures of each child. Glue each photograph to a 3-inch square of construction paper. Cover with clear self-stick paper for durability, if desired. Turn all of the squares face down. Let the children take turns turning over two squares at a time to find matching pairs. Have the children name who is in each picture as they turn the squares over.

Hint: If you have professional class pictures taken, use the proofs of the children to make this game.

It's Fun to Get to Know You

Sung to: "Did You Ever See a Lassie?"

It's fun to get to know you,
To know you, to know you,
It's fun to get to know you,
And be your friend.
To play with, to work with,
To have so much fun with.
It's fun to get to know you,
And be your friend.

Patricia Coyne

Cooperative Treasure Hunt

Hide treats, such as small boxes of raisins or seasonal stickers in various places around the room. Draw a picture of each place that a treat is hidden. Cut each picture into four puzzle pieces. Divide the children into groups. Give each group a puzzle. Have the groups put their puzzles together to find out where their treats are hidden.

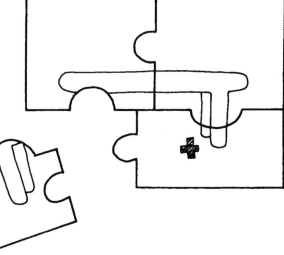

Cooperative Quilt

Give each child a long strip of adding machine tape. Let the children use crayons or felt-tip markers to decorate their strips as desired. Hang half of the decorated strips vertically on a wall or a bulletin board. Weave the remaining strips horizontally over and under the hanging strips, taping them in place as needed.

Hint: Purchase rolls of adding machine tape at office supply stores or check with a local business about collecting used tape.

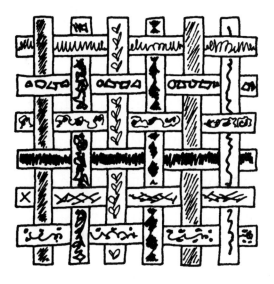

Friends

Have the children sit in a circle and ask them this question: "How can you tell if someone likes you?" Let the children brainstorm answers. Some possible responses might be:

"They ask you to play; They smile at you; They share; They sit near you; They hold your hand; They giggle with you; They do nice things for you."

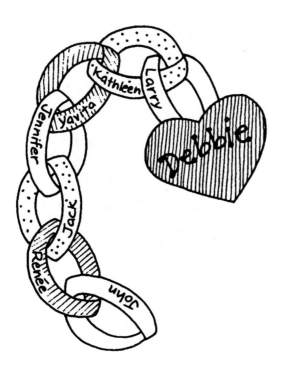

Friendship Chains

Let each child glue colorful strips of paper together to make a chain. At one end of the chain, staple a paper heart shape with the child's name printed on it. Then ask the child to name his or her friends. As the child does so, print the names on the loops of his or her chain. Encourage the children to talk about their friends and the things they like to do with them as they make their chains.

Won't You Be a Friend Of Mine?

Sung to: "The Muffin Man"

Oh, won't you be a friend of mine,
A friend of mine, a friend of mine?
Oh, won't you be a friend of mine
And play with me today?

Yes, I'll be a friend of yours,
A friend of yours, a friend of yours.
Yes, I'll be a friend of yours
And play with you today.

Julie Israel

My Friend

Ask the children what they like to do with their friends. Then sing the following song, substituting one of those activities for the phrase *plays in the sand with me.*

Sung to: "The Wheels on the Bus"

My friend plays in the sand with me,
The sand with me, the sand with me.
My friend plays in the sand with me
Every day at school.

Betty Silkunas

Stranger Collage

Set out magazines, glue and pieces of construction paper. Ask the children to look through the magazines and tear out pictures of people who they would call strangers. Then let them glue the pictures onto their pieces of construction paper. Make a picture collage yourself, being sure to include pictures of people the children might normally see but who are still strangers, such as nurses, construction workers or grocery store clerks. Let the children share their collages. Ask them to talk about why they chose the pictures they did. Show them your collage. Reinforce during the shar-

ing that a stranger is anyone they do not know and that they should never get in a car with, or otherwise follow a stranger, no matter what the person says. Remind the children that the rule is: Never go with anyone without telling your parent or guardian first.

Safe People Art

Talk with the children about "safe" people. Tell them that a safe person is someone you can share a scary secret with, even if you've been told not to tell. A scary secret might be that you saw a big kid take a little kid's lunchbox, and the big kid told you not to tell or he'd take your lunchbox too. Then give them felt-tip markers and pieces of construction paper. Ask the children to draw pictures of all the people they know who are safe. Have each child talk about the people in his or her picture. Ask the children what they would do if the first one or two people they told their scary secret to did not listen. Introduce the concept of "Keep on telling."

Families Tree

Cut a large tree shape out of brown butcher paper. Hang the tree shape on a wall or a bulletin board at the children's eye level. Have the children draw pictures of their families on pieces of construction paper. Help them write the names of their family members on their papers. Then let them attach their pictures to the tree shape to make your "Families Tree."

Variation: Have each child bring in a photo of his or her family to attach to the tree.

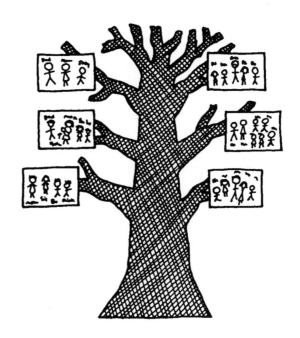

Family Packets

Give each child an extra-large envelope. Let the children decorate the outsides of their envelopes as desired. Have them take their envelopes home to use for compiling packets of family information. Encourage the children and their families to include such things as names of family members, brief descriptions of recent family outings, names of favorite foods, descriptions of special cultural celebrations and customs, and family photos. Have one child each day share his or her packet. Let the child talk about the pictures, who is in his or her family, etc. Set aside a special place to display all of the children's packets.

Family Dress-Up

Ask the children to bring in some of their family's old clothes. Put the clothes in your dress-up area. Let the children dress up in the clothes and pretend that they are different people in their families.

I'm Glad I Have a Family

Sung to: "Did You Ever See a Lassie?"

I'm glad I have a family,
A family, a family,
I'm glad I have a family,
A family to love.
With Mommy and Daddy
And Sister and Brother.
I'm glad I have a family,
A family to love.

Substitute the names of the members of one of your children's families for *Mommy, Daddy, Sister* and *Brother.*

Neoma Kreuter

Guess Who's Talking?

Have the children's family members tape-record short messages for the group. Play the messages one at a time and have the children try to guess who is talking.

Hello, kids...

Rock Families

Have each child collect four or five different sized rocks to make a "family." Then let the children play "house" with their rocks. Encourage them to make up stories about their rock families. For example, have them name their rocks and tell what each one likes to do. Or have them tell about how their rock families celebrate special occasions such as birthdays or Thanksgiving. Help them to expand their stories by asking questions.

Variation: Instead of rocks, let the children use different sized buttons or wood blocks to create families.

Helping Hands Book

Explain to the children that being a part of a family means doing chores and helping out in any way they can. Ask them to tell you of ways they help out in their families. Then let them make helping hands books to give to their parents. Make paint pads by placing folded paper towels in shallow containers and pouring on small amounts of tempera paint. Give each child five or six pieces of white construction paper. Have each child gently press his or her hand on a paint pad, then press it once on each of his or her papers. (Have a tub of warm soapy water and some towels ready for the children to use for cleaning their hands.) Let the children decorate construction paper covers on which you have written, "Whenever there is work to do, just tear out a hand and I'll help you." Then complete each child's book by stapling his or her pages and cover together.

Helper Charts

Let the children choose chores they can do at home to help out. Then give each child a piece of paper with seven boxes drawn on it and the name of his or her selcted chore written on it. Have the child's parents draw a star in a box each time their child does the chore. When all the boxes are filled in, have the child bring the chart back to you to exchange for a small treat such as a sticker or a colored pencil.

Puppy Polite

Let the children make Puppy Polite puppets. Give them each a paper bag. Have them use felt-tip markers or crayons to draw dog faces on the flaps of their bags. Then give each child two dog ear shapes to glue onto the sides of his or her bag. Have the children use their puppets when you talk about manners. Ask them to tell about all the polite things Puppy Polite knows how to do, such as covering his nose when he sneezes, saying please and thank you and waiting quietly in line. Whenever there is a question about manners, ask the children what they think Puppy Polite would do.

When You Talk to People

Sung to: "Did You Ever See a Lassie?"

When you talk to people,
You should use good manners,
When you talk to people,
You should be polite.
When they say, "Thank you,"
Then you say, "You're welcome."
When you talk to people,
You should be polite.

When you talk to people,
You should use good manners,
When you talk to people,
You should be polite.
When they say, "How are you?"
Then you say, "Fine, thank you."
When you talk to people,
You should be polite.

Jean D. Smith

Problem Solving

Ask "What if?" questions about sharing problems that commonly arise and help the children come up with positive solutions. For example, ask: "What if you want to play on the swing but your friend won't get off? What if you're starting a game and both you and your friend want to be first? What if there's one cookie left and three of you want it?" Encourage the children to bring up other problems for the group to try solving.

We Share

Sung to: "Twinkle, Twinkle, Little Star"

We share all our blocks and toys
With the other girls and boys.
Crayons, scissors, paint and glue,
Puzzles, books, the easel, too.
We take turns because it's fair,
And we're happy when we share.

Sue Brown

Sharing Toys

When there are more children than one type of toy, such as riding toys or puzzles, try this solution. Play some music while the children are using those toys. At the end of each song, have each child with that kind of toy give it to a child who has not yet played with it. Repeat for as long as playtime lasts.

Share Your Toys
Sung to: "Row, Row, Row Your Boat"

Share, share, share your toys,
Share them with your friends.
It's so much fun to share your toys,
Sharing has no end.

Let's all share our toys,
Let's share them with our friends.
It's so much fun to share our toys,
Sharing has no end.

Rosemary Giordano

Gift Boxes

Use this activity to help the children practice giving and receiving gifts. Set out empty gift boxes, sheets of newspaper and tape. Let each child wrap one of the boxes with newspaper. Have the children sit in a circle with their boxes. Let one child at a time give his or her box to another child. Have that child unwrap the box and thank the giver for the "present" inside. Repeat until each child has had a chance to be a giver and a receiver.

Kind Words

Sung to: "Skip to My Lou"

It's nice to say thank you,
It's nice to say thank you,
It's nice to say think you,
When someone's kind to you.

Judith Taylor Burtchet

Rocking Chair Talk

Arrange a large comfortable rocking chair in a special place in your room. Tell the children that whenever they have a problem or something they would like to discuss with you, they should sit in the chair and you will join them as soon as you can. This is a wonderful way to encourage the children to ask for help when they need it and to model caring behavior.

Caring Cards

Let the children make greeting cards using their choice of a variety of art media. Then deliver the cards (or let the children help you deliver them) to a nursing home, a senior center or to homes in your neighborhood.

Birthday Scroll

A Birthday Scroll is an excellent way for children to show that they care about each other. When it is a child's birthday, set out a long piece of paper. Let the children tear or cut out pictures that illustrate their feelings about the birthday child. Have them paste the pictures on the roll of paper. Help the children sign their names to the scroll, then give it to the birthday child.

Variation: Instead of making a Birthday Scroll, you could let the children make a Get Well Scroll, a Cheer-Up Scroll, a Congratulations Scroll, etc.

Share and Care Book

Talk with the children about the meaning of sharing and caring. Then give each child a piece of paper. Let the children draw or glue on magazine pictures that illustrate how they share with and care for their friends. Have the children dictate sentences about their pictures for you to write down. Laminate or cover each page with clear self-stick paper for durability. Add a cover page with the title "We Share and Care." Punch holes in the pages and insert metal rings. Read the completed book out loud, then place it where the children can look through it by themselves.

Extension: As the children do new activities to demonstrate sharing and caring, add new pages to your book.

Goodwill Day

Have the children bring in un-
wanted toys and books to give to
needy children in your area. (Stress
that the items should be in good
condition.) Let the children help
take the toys and books to an orga-
nization that can properly distribute
them to those in need. Or have one
of the organizations come to your
room and pick up the items.

Variation: Organize a Toy Drive. Let
the children collect toys and books
from families in their neighbor-
hoods. Get together for a Repair
Day to clean and fix up the items.

Caring Tree

Stand a tree branch in a pot of soil.
Ask the children to name ways they
can show love or kindness to others,
such as helping to put away toys,
setting the table or sharing crayons
with friends. Then have each child
dictate a sentence to you telling how
he or she will show love or kindness
to someone else. Print each child's
sentence on a separate construction
paper heart shape. Hang the hearts
on the tree branch with string or
yarn to create a Caring Tree.

Dear Parents,

We are learning about families, the people in them and what families do. Try doing the following activities together with your family and share some special times.

Choose Days

Designate a special day each month or week as "Choose Day." On that morning or afternoon, let one family member determine how the entire family will spend the time. Since everyone gets to choose a special activity eventually, complaints about choices are rare.

Travel Talk

Time spent in the car can be quality time if family members spend it talking and sharing. Not only do the miles go faster, but many new lessons can be learned. Some ideas for Travel Talk are as follows: "What day would you most like to live over? What would you like to do in the future? What foods would you order if you were at a restaurant and could afford anything? What would you buy first if you won a million dollars?"

Family Album

Let your child make his or her own family album. Have your child draw a picture of each person in the family on a separate page. Encourage your child to include on each page a few pictures of that person's favorite things. You could help your child cover the album with fabric and find a place of honor for the book with your other family albums.

Dear Parents,

We have been learning about ways to show we care about other people. Find ways to show that you and your child care about others by doing the following activities together.

Home Visit

Go with your child and visit a friend or neighbor who is shut-in or someone in a nursing home. Let your child draw a picture or make a card to take along. Talk about how it would feel to have to be inside all day long and what it would feel like to have company. If desired, make your visit a regular weekly or monthly activity.

Sharing With Others

Place a large basket on a table where everyone can see it. Each time you and your child go to the grocery store, let your child pick out a can of food to put in the basket. When the basket is full, let your child help you take it to your local food bank.

Building Self-Esteem

Play this game to help build the self-esteem of your child and to teach him or her how to build the self-esteem of others. Select one family member to start with. Have the other family members each tell one thing they like about what that person does. For example: "I like it when you let me play with your doll; when you pick up your toys without being told; when you tell funny jokes." Repeat for each family member.

Getting to Know Others
Contributors

Ideas in this chapter were contributed by:

Janice Bodenstedt, Jackson, MI
Sue Brown, Louisville, KY
Judith Taylor Burtchet, El Dorado, KS
Juliane Churetta, Coplay, PA
Sarah Cooper, Arlington, TX
Patricia Coyne, Mansfield, MA
Diana L. Delp, Quakertown, PA
Rosemary Giordano, Philadelphia, PA
Rene Gutyan, Williams Lake, B.C.
Janice Hill, Coaldale, PA
LoriAnn Hoober, Kutztown, PA
Joan Hunter, Elbridge, NY
Julie Israel, Ypsilanti, MI
Ellen Javernick, Loveland, CO
Lisa Johnson, Dubuque, IA
Neoma Kreuter, Ontario, CA
Donna Mullennix, Thousand Oaks, CA
Paula Omlin, Maple Valley, WA
Lois Putnam, Pilot Mt., NC
Bev Qualheim, Marquette, MI
Vicki Reynolds, East Hanover, NJ
Jill Semmel, Lehighton, PA
Betty Silkunas, Lansdale, PA
Jean D. Smith, Huron, OH
Shari Steelsmith, Bothell, WA

Reproducible
Patterns

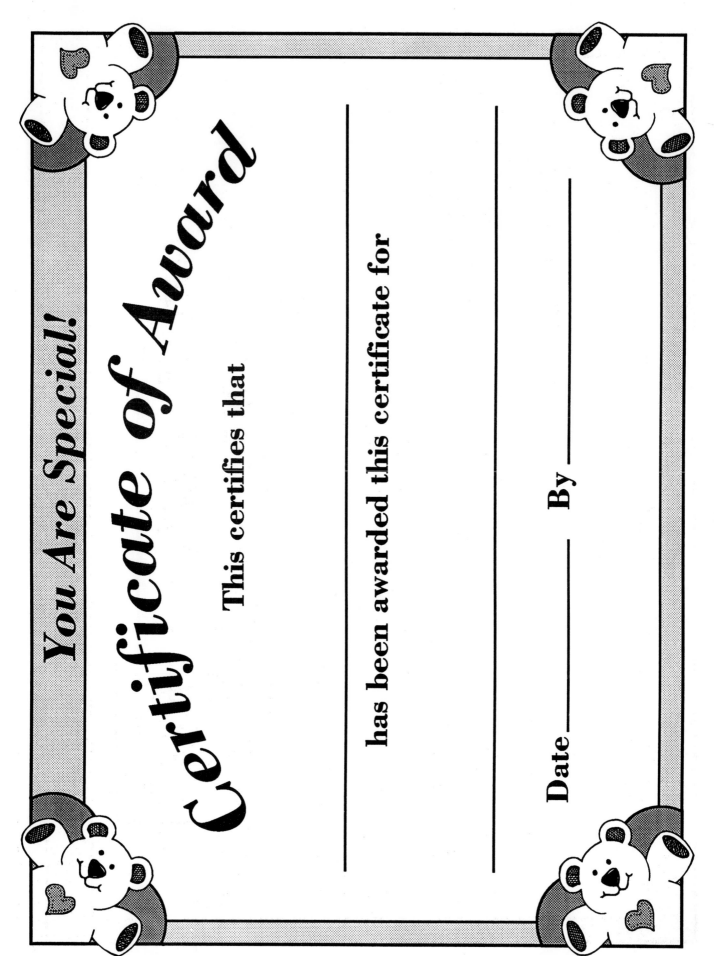

You Are Special!

Certificate of Award

This certifies that

has been awarded this certificate for

By _____

Date _____

Certificate of Birth

Name _____

Date of Birth _____

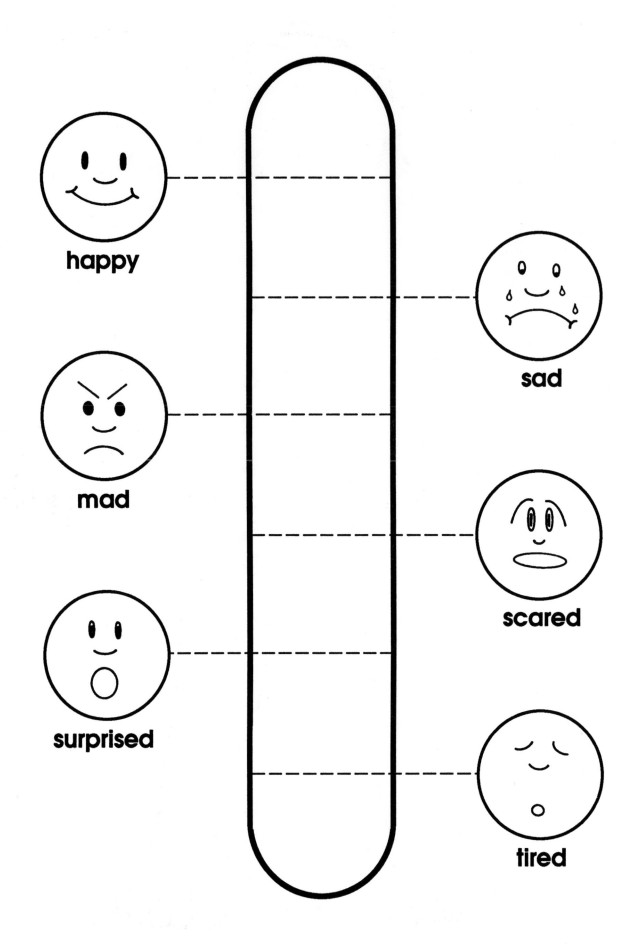

happy

sad

mad

scared

surprised

tired

See activity on page 32 for directions.

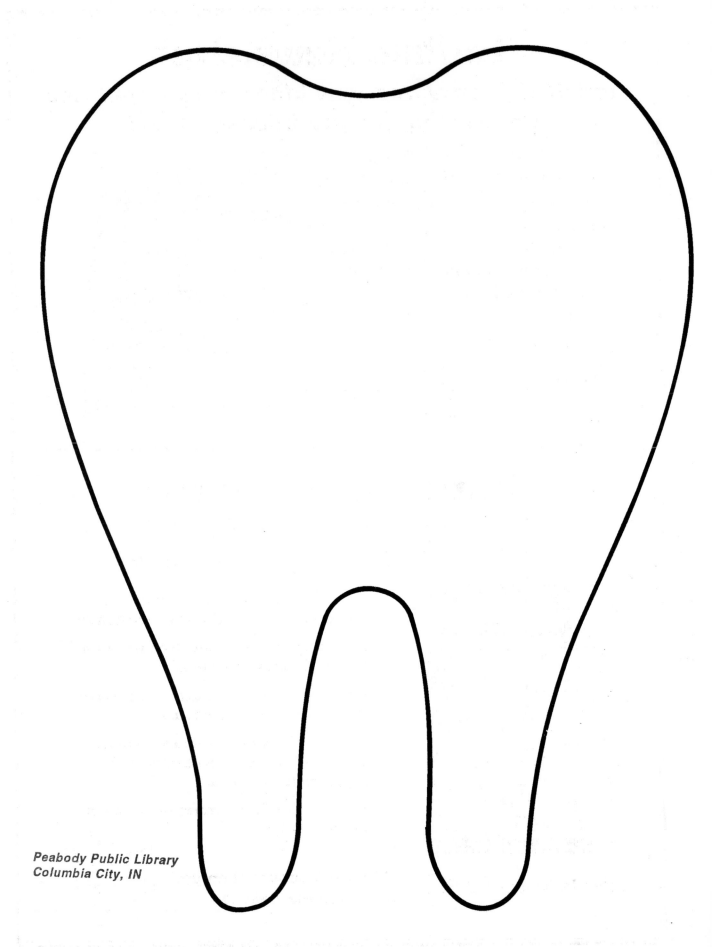

78 *Tooth*

See activities on pages 43 and 44 for directions.

Totline® Newsletter

Activities, songs and new ideas to use right now are waiting for you in every issue!

Each issue puts the fun into teaching with 32 pages of challenging and creative activities for young children. Included are open-ended art activities, learning games, music, language and science activities plus 8 reproducible pattern pages.

Published bi-monthly.

Sample issue - $2.00

Super Snack News

Nutritious snack ideas, related songs, rhymes and activities

Teach young children health and nutrition through fun and creative activities.

- Use as a handout to involve parents in their children's education.

- Promote quality child care in the community with these handouts.

- Includes nutritious sugarless snacks, health tidbits, and developmentally appropriate activities.

- Includes CACFP information for most snacks.

Sample issue - $2.00

With each subscription you are given the right to:

Make up to:
200 COPIES
per issue

Warren Publishing House, Inc. • P.O. Box 2250, Dept. Z • Everett, WA 98203